First World War
and Army of Occupation
War Diary
France, Belgium and Germany

24 DIVISION
Divisional Troops
A Squadron Glasgow Yeomanry
31 August 1915 - 30 April 1916

WO95/2197/1

The Naval & Military Press Ltd
www.nmarchive.com
Published in association with The National Archives

Published by

The Naval & Military Press Ltd

Unit 10 Ridgewood Industrial Park,

Uckfield, East Sussex,

TN22 5QE England

Tel: +44 (0) 1825 749494

www.naval-military-press.com

www.nmarchive.com

This diary has been reprinted in facsimile from the original. Any imperfections are inevitably reproduced and the quality may fall short of modern type and cartographic standards.

© **Crown Copyright**
Images reproduced by permission of The National Archives, London, England, 2015.

Contents

Document type	Place/Title	Date From	Date To
Heading	WO95/2197-1		
Heading	'A' SQN Glasgow Yeomanry Sep 1915-Apr 1916		
Heading	24th Division		
Heading	War Diary Of "A" Squadron Q.O.R. Glasgow Yeomanry From 31st August 1915 to 30 September 1915		
War Diary	Cowshott Camp Bisley	31/08/1915	31/08/1915
War Diary	Havre	01/09/1915	01/09/1915
War Diary	Hesmond	02/09/1915	20/09/1915
War Diary	Laires	21/09/1915	21/09/1915
War Diary	Busnes	22/09/1915	23/09/1915
War Diary	Annezin	24/09/1915	26/09/1915
War Diary	Vermelles	26/09/1915	26/09/1915
War Diary	Sailly-Labourse	27/09/1915	28/09/1915
War Diary	St. Hillaire	29/09/1915	30/09/1915
Heading	24th Division "a" Squadron Glasgow Yeo: Vol: 2 Oct. 15		
Heading	War Diary of "A" Squadron Q.O.R. Glasgow Yeomanry From 1st October 1915 To 31st October 1915: Vol II.		
War Diary	St. Hilaire	01/10/1915	01/10/1915
War Diary	Wallon Cappel	02/10/1915	02/10/1915
War Diary	Herzeele	03/10/1915	05/10/1915
War Diary	Boeschepe	06/10/1915	31/10/1915
Heading	24th Division "A" Sq. Glasgow Yeo Vol.3 Nov 15		
War Diary	Boeschepe	01/11/1915	22/11/1915
War Diary	Hardifort	23/11/1915	25/11/1915
War Diary	Tilques	26/11/1915	27/11/1915
War Diary	Salperwick	28/11/1915	30/11/1915
Heading	24th Division "A" Sq Glasgow Yeo Vol: 4		
War Diary	Salperwick	01/12/1915	31/12/1915
Heading	A Sp. G'sow Yeo Vol 5		
Heading	War Diary of "A" Squadron Q.O.R. Glasgow Yeomanry from 1.1.16 to 31.1.16		
War Diary	St. Martin (Salperwick)	01/01/1916	05/01/1916
War Diary	Steenevoorde	06/01/1916	06/01/1916
War Diary	Poperinghe (Camp 3miles S.W. of P.)	07/01/1916	13/01/1916
War Diary	Poperinghe	14/01/1916	31/01/1916
Heading	War. Diary Of "A" Squadron Q.O.R. Glasgow Yeomanry 24th Division. From 1st Feby to 29th Feby 1916		
Miscellaneous	a Sp. G'sow Yeo: Vol. 6		
War Diary	Poperinghe (Camp 3 miles S.W. of P.)	01/02/1916	05/02/1916
War Diary	Poperinghe	06/02/1916	29/02/1916
Heading	War Diary 24 of "A" Squadron Q.O.R. Glasgow Yeomanry 24th Division From 1st March to 31st March 1916		
War Diary	Poperinghe	01/03/1916	30/03/1916
War Diary	Bailleul	31/03/1916	31/03/1916

War Diary	War Diary of "A" Squadron Q.O.R. Glasgow Yeomanry from 1st April To 30th April 1916 Vol. VIII		
War Diary	Bailleul	01/04/1916	28/04/1916
War Diary	Renescure	29/04/1916	29/04/1916
War Diary	Val D'Acquin	30/04/1916	30/04/1916
War Diary			

woods/2/97 |1

**24TH DIVISION
DIVL TROOPS**

'A' SQN GLASGOW YEOMANRY
SEP 1915 - APR 1916

To 5 CORPS

131/7083

34th Division

"A" Squadron Lovats Yeomanry

Vol: I

Sept. 15
Apr. '16

CONFIDENTIAL

WAR DIARY
of
"A" SQUADRON
Q.O.R. GLASGOW YEOMANRY

from
31st August 1915
to
30 September 1915

Volume I.

PAGE 1

Army Form C. 2118.

Instructions regarding War Diaries and Intelligence Summaries are contained in F.S. Regs., Part II. and the Staff Manual respectively. Title pages will be prepared in manuscript.

WAR DIARY
— or —
INTELLIGENCE SUMMARY.
(Erase heading not required.) "A" Squadron QUEENS OWN ROYAL GLASGOW YEOMANRY

Hour, Date, Place	Summary of Events and Information	Remarks and references to Appendices
31st August 1915 COWSHOTT CAMP BISLEY	In conformity with orders received from H.Q. 24th Division, the squadron left camp at 1:30 A.M. to entrain at BROOKWOOD STATION. 1st Train with ½ squadron left at 3.35 A.M. and arrived SOUTHHAMPTON at 5:45 A.M. 2nd Train left at 5:30 A.M. and arrived SOUTHHAMPTON at 7.40 A.M. Total strength of squadron on entrained — 5 Officers, 129 other ranks. 150 horses, under command of Major H.R. CAYZER. Details left at Camp – 1 officer and 11 other ranks. 1 man left behind in hospital. Veterinary inspection at SOUTHHAMPTON. 9 horses exchanged. Embarked on S.S. NIRVANA at 8:30 A.M. Cleared SOUTHHAMPTON at 5 P.M. Col. BUTCHER R.A. in command of ship.	
1st September HAVRE	Calm crossing. Arrived HAVRE at 4 A.M. Disembarked at 7 A.M. and proceeded to GARE MARITIME. Casualties on board ship — 3 horses – colic. 1 horse – Pneumonia and 1 Kicked. Drew 5 in exchange from Remount Depot and 1 to make up establishment. Interpreter attached himself and was attached to squadron. Entrained and left GARE MARITIME at 9.40 P.M.	
2nd September HESMOND	Arrived at MARESQUEL 12.30 P.M. Detrained and proceeded by march to HESMOND. Troops billeted in 4 farms. Horses picketed in open. H.Q. of Division at ROYON 4 kilometres E of HESMOND	
3rd September "	Very heavy rain all day. Horse lines became very soft. Horses put under shelter in farms. T.L.G.	

WAR DIARY
INTELLIGENCE SUMMARY.
(Erase heading not required.)

Army Form C. 2118.

PAGE 2

Hour, Date, Place	Summary of Events and Information	Remarks and references to Appendices
4th September to 19th September HESMOND	Two weeks of fine weather. Squadron training continued, the Squadron taking part in ceremonial Divisional reviews. The 21st Division together with the 21st and the Guards Division to form the 11th Corps under the command of General HAKING. On Sunday 13th 1 NCO and 6 men (escort) proceeded to H.Q. XIth Corps at ST OMER. T.9.	
20th September HESMOND	Orders received that the Division is moving on enemy at 21st. One officer and 15 other ranks attached as escort to Divisional H.Q.	2/Lt MURRAY
21st September LAIRES	Left HESMOND at 5.30 PM. Attached to 73rd INF BDE. for billeting purposes. Joined BDE at ROYON and marched via FRUGES to LAIRES arriving at 11 PM. Divisional H.Q. at BOMY.	
22nd September BUSNES	Left LAIRES at 6 PM. Marched via ST HILAIRE to BUSNES. Arrived at 10 PM.	
23rd " "	Rested at BUSNES. Weather during the march from HESMOND very good - warm during the day and bright moonlight at night. T.9.	

WAR DIARY
INTELLIGENCE SUMMARY.

(Erase heading not required.)

Army Form C. 2118.

PAGE 3

Hour, Date, Place	Summary of Events and Information	Remarks and references to Appendices
24th September ANNEZIN	Detached from 93rd Inf Bde. Left BUSNES at 6.30 P.M. and proceeded to billets in ANNEZIN. Divisional H.Q. at Rue Gambetta, BETHUNE.	
25th September	Divisional H.Q. moved to VERMELLES. The Squadron ordered to report to 9th Division at SAILLY-LABOURSE. Reported there and joined up with "B" Squadron, GLASGOW YEOMANRY at 5 P.M. Very heavy rain came on during the afternoon. At 6 P.M. previous orders cancelled and squadron ordered to proceed at once to VERMELLES and report to H.Q. 24th Div. Arrived at VERMELLES 7.30 P.M. Village being shelled. Orders received to go to CROSS ROADS 2 Kilometres S.W. of VERMELLES and wait with Reserve in rear of SHERWOOD FORESTERS. The direction of the advance to be EAST along path from CROSS ROADS towards HULLUCH. Started out from VERMELLES at 8 P.M. Road to CROSS ROADS badly blocked by Motor Ambulance Waggons going both ways and Cookers. Progress very slow. Arrived at CROSS ROADS at 9.30 P.M. SHERWOOD FORESTERS reported	

PAGE 4

WAR DIARY
INTELLIGENCE SUMMARY.
(Erase heading not required.)

Army Form C. 2118.

Hour, Date, Place	Summary of Events and Information	Remarks and references to Appendices
	to have gone along the path toward HULLUCH. Squadron followed on. Ground flat and often badly cut up by lines of trenches which had been bridged over in places by narrow wooden bridges. The heavy ground soaked with recent rain, expectation of the traffic over the bridges and the lack of any daylight made leading very difficult. In the dark about to join the Squadron which was dug in among a few still live shells dropping from the NE and also SE from the direction of LOOS. After proceeding about 200 yards the SHERWOOD FORESTERS could not be found and it was not known where the Reserve was. As it would have been injudicious for the Squadron to have gone further and so he left in the exposed position at dawn the order to counter-march was given. On returning to the Cross Roads the SHERWOOD FORESTERS were found to be in the Reserve trenches there.	
26th September	Remained at the Cross Roads till 2 A.M. when orders were received from Division H.Q. to retire to COURANT-LE-BULLY. Retired through VERMELLES and halted at Cross Roads 1 Kilometre NW of VERMELLES. 9 A.M. Squadron on road ready to move off.	

PAGE 5

Army Form C. 2118.

WAR DIARY
or
INTELLIGENCE SUMMARY.

(Erase heading not required.)

Hour, Date, Place	Summary of Events and Information	Remarks and references to Appendices
26th September 9 A.M. VERMELLES	Major CAYZER proceeded to H.Q. in VERMELLES to receive orders. On going along the street his horse was badly hit by a shell and had to be destroyed. Two officers (2nd Lt WILSON and 2nd Lt DONALDSON) sent out to the Cross Roads 2 Kilometres SW of VERMELLES to carry dispatches from H.Q. to the firing line holding the first line of GERMAN trenches in front of HULLUCH. Squadron remained in readiness all day. At night made N.W. of VERMELLES picketed to collect stragglers and disabled troops returning from the trenches to the concentration point. T.B. 10 a.m. Went into billets at SAILLY-LABOURSE.	
27th September SAILLY-LABOURSE		
28th September	Suddenly ordered to leave SAILLY. Very hot duty night. Left SAILLY at 8.30 P.M. Billeted at 11 P.M at ANNEZIN along with Mounted Troops of the Division less R.A.	

PAGE 6

Army Form C. 2118.

WAR DIARY
INTELLIGENCE SUMMARY.
(Erase heading not required.)

Hour, Date, Place	Summary of Events and Information	Remarks and references to Appendices
29th September St HILLAIRE	Left ANNEZIN at 11 A.M. Went via LILLERS to St. HILLAIRE and then billeted.	
30th September	Rested for day in St HILLAIRE T.S.	

M/7517

34th Division

"A" Squadron Naafus Yeo:
Vol: 2
Oct. 15

CONFIDENTIAL

WAR DIARY
of
"A" Squadron Q.O.R.
Glasgow Yeomanry

From 1st October 1915.
To 31st October 1915.

Vol. II.

Vol. II Page 1

WAR DIARY
INTELLIGENCE SUMMARY.
(Erase heading not required.)

Army Form C. 2118.

Hour, Date, Place	Summary of Events and Information	Remarks and references to Appendices
1st October 1915 ST HILAIRE	Squadron left ST HILAIRE at 10.15AM and marched via LAMBRES – THIENNES arriving at WALLON CAPPEL at 1.30 PM Billeted for the night.	
2nd Oct WALLON CAPPEL	Moved from billets at 9am, marched via CASSEL to HERZEELE arrived at 1 P.M. and billeted.	
3rd Oct – 5th Oct HERZEELE	3rd Oct – Rested at HERZEELE. 4th Oct – Squadron 80 men strong, proceeded to GODEWAERSVELDE to collect Remounts for the various units of the Division. Arrived at 6 P.M. and obtained 234 horses and mules in the dark. The Artillery and Divisional Train Horse parties failed to arrive to take over their horses and it was necessary to lead all the horses back to HERZEELE which was reached at 11 P.M. and there the remounts were linked in a field. Orders received from Divisional H.Q. at STEENVOORDE to proceed to BOESCHEPE on the following morning. 5th Oct. 7am. – Sorted out Remounts and handed over a few to the units who came to collect them. Squadron left HERZEELE at 11AM taking 50 Remounts (mules) for the Artillery and leaving the remainder (L.D, H.D. and mules) in the field under the charge of the Divisional Train. Marched via STEENVOORDE and arrived at BOESCHEPE at 2 P.M.	

PAGE 2.

WAR DIARY
or
INTELLIGENCE SUMMARY.
(Erase heading not required.)

Army Form C. 2118.

Hour, Date, Place	Summary of Events and Information	Remarks and references to Appendices
5th Oct 1915	The 4th Division now belonging to the 5th Corps, an escort consisting of 2nd Lieut Wilson and 17 other ranks, was detailed to report to the Camp Commandant at ABEELE on the 6th Oct for duty under 5th Corps H.Q. One riding horse sent to 36th Mobile Veterinary Section and struck off the strength of Squadron.	
6th Oct BOESCHEPE	Billeted in BOESCHEPE. 4 Riding and 2 Light Draught horses taken on strength of Squadron to relieve shortage. The Remounts being Ur from HERZEELE, handed over to Artillery.	
7th Oct	Escort of 5 men previously attached to 11th Corps H.Q. returned to Squadron.	
8th Oct	One riding horse sent to 36th Mobile Vet Sect. 2nd Troop detailed to act as Divisional Salvage Corps under command of 2nd Lt DONALDSON. Squadron inspected by General CAPPER, the new Divisional Commander of 24th Division. He gave a good report on the condition and turn out of the Squadron.	

PAGE 3

Army Form C. 2118.

WAR DIARY
or
INTELLIGENCE SUMMARY.
(Erase heading not required.)

Instructions regarding War Diaries and Intelligence Summaries are contained in F.S. Regs., Part II. and the Staff Manual respectively. Title pages will be prepared in manuscript.

Hour, Date, Place	Summary of Events and Information	Remarks and references to Appendices
9th Oct. BOESCHEPE	Hot bath provided for the men at the Brewery under supervision of 7th Field Ambulance. Clean underclothing given where necessary.	
10th – 13th Oct.		
14th Oct.	1 N.C.O. and 4 men detailed to police the town of BOESCHEPE.	
	One officer and 3 men detailed to attend funeral of an escort RENINGHELST for interment of bodies of drowned troops.	
15th Oct.	One Sergeant and 12 men ordered to report to A.P.M. 5th Corps ABEELE for permanent duty at fortis control post.	
16th – 17th Oct.		
17th Oct.	Took over billets and stables vacated by "A" Squadron Yorkshire Dragoons 17th Div. & handed to WINNEZEELE Stables consist of 7.15	

(9 29 6) W 4141—453 100,000 9/14 H W V Forms/C. 2118/10

PAGE 4

WAR DIARY
or
INTELLIGENCE SUMMARY.
(Erase heading not required.)

Army Form C. 2118.

Hour, Date, Place	Summary of Events and Information	Remarks and references to Appendices
1st Oct. BOESCHEPE	Built shelter for with flatted roofs and tarfelt built of two long buildings (unfinished) 170 feet x 30 ft. and screen on N.E. side.	
19th – 31st Oct.	The work of completing stables & huts for Winter Quarters proceeded with. As ground was very soft and muddy large quantities of bricks and sand had to be carted from ST JANS CAPPEL for flooring stables and making roads. Wood for building huts supplied from C.R.E. RENINGHELST.	
22nd Oct.	Four patrols of two men each sent out on Survey duty to report on condition of the roads in 24th Divisional area. From these a took a map of the roads constructed and sent to H.Q.	
23rd Oct.	2nd Lieutenant A. McCulloch (Supernumerary) TRS	

PAGE 5

Army Form C. 2118.

WAR DIARY
INTELLIGENCE SUMMARY.
(Erase heading not required.)

Hour, Date, Place	Summary of Events and Information	Remarks and references to Appendices
23rd Oct. BOESCHEPE	transferred to "B" Squadron Q.V.R. Glasgow Yeomanry	
26th Oct	Ceremonial parade at RENINGHELST on account of inspection of the Troops by the King. Squadron represented by 16 men forming part of a composite battalion from the 9th Cav. Div.	
28th Oct	One horse being evacuated sick to Britain in strength off strength of squadron.	
29th Oct	Squadron horses inspected by D.D.R. 5th Corps. Very pleased with condition of horses and stated they were about the best he had seen. He also commented on the good shoeing.	

PAGE 6

WAR DIARY
or
INTELLIGENCE SUMMARY.
(Erase heading not required.)

Army Form C. 2118.

Hour, Date, Place	Summary of Events and Information	Remarks and references to Appendices
31 Oct. BOESCHEPE	Major CAYZER, Capt. GALLOWAY and Lt GOW left the front line trenches preceded by Capt. DIENEBUSCH & about 1 1/2 S.W. of YPRES. Hence on foot across Canal and via YPRES - St ELOI Road to LANKHOF CHATEAU and then S.E. to the BLUFF trenches.	left 1st February 1915

24th November

"A" Sq: Q'SM Yes.
Vol. 3

131/
7795

Nov 15

Vol. III Page 1

Army Form C. 2118.

WAR DIARY
INTELLIGENCE SUMMARY

(Erase heading not required.)

Hour, Date, Place	Summary of Events and Information	Remarks and references to Appendices
BOESCHEPE		
1st Nov. 1915	Work of building stables proceeding	
2nd Nov.	Routine as usual.	
	One man being discharged from hospital is taken on Strength of Squadron	
	Sergt and 6 other ranks rejoin Squadron from divisional H.Q. Escort.	T.L.G.
3rd Nov.	Routine T.L.G.	
4th Nov.	Routine T.L.G.	
5th Nov.	Routine T.L.G.	
6th Nov.	Routine T.L.G.	
7th Nov.	Routine T.L.	
8th Nov.	Routine as.	
	Sergts ALLANT and ALEXANDER J. having refused to sign on after termination of their period of service proceeded to Base for discharge and are struck off strength of Squadron. T.L.G.	
9th Nov.	Routine as usual T.L.G	

WAR DIARY or INTELLIGENCE SUMMARY

Hour, Date, Place	Summary of Events and Information	Remarks and references to Appendices
BOESCHEPE 10th Nov. 11th Nov.	Routine as hand. T.L.R. The following promotions were made this day. Sergt Robertson to be Sergt. Cpl. Fleming to be Sergt. Cpl. Christie to be L/Sergt. L/Cpl. Gordon to be Corporal. L/Cpl. Reardon to be Corporal. Pmv L/Cpl Somer to be L/Cpl. Pmv. L/Cpl Hamilton to be L/Cpl. Pte. Galloway to be Pmv. L/Cpl. Pte. McKied to be Pmv. L/Cpl.	T.L.R.
12th Nov.	2nd Lieut. K.C. Murray seconded, to date from 9.10.15, having been attached A.P.C. to Major General J.E. Capper CB. 24th Div., and this attachment having been approved by 5th Corps memo SM/3825 dated 8/11/15. Orders today received from H.Q. 24th Div. Major Cayzer and Capt. Galloway proceeded to VOORMEZEELE via DICKEBUSCH and CAFÉ BELGE to arrange about placing two observation posts for the purpose of observing all movement to behind German trenches. Road leading to VOORMEZEELE from CAFÉ BELGE	

PAGE III

Army Form C. 2118.

WAR DIARY
INTELLIGENCE SUMMARY

(Erase heading not required.)

Instructions regarding War Diaries and Intelligence Summaries are contained in F. S. Regs., Part II. and the Staff Manual respectively. Title pages will be prepared in manuscript.

Hour, Date, Place	Summary of Events and Information	Remarks and references to Appendices
BOESCHEPE 12th Nov (Cont)	Very heavily shelled. The following NCOs and men transferred to Divl. HQ for duty at observation posts at VOORMEZEELE and proceeded there:- No I Post {Sergt. McNAUGHTON D. Pte. GENTLEMAN T. " JOHNSTON T. No II Post {Cpl. REEMAN A. Pte. GRIER E. " PINCHON H.W.	
13th Nov	Routine as usual. T.L.	
14th Nov	Routine " " T.L. 4 men proceeded to RENINGHELST for duty with A.P.M. 2nd Div. T.L.	
15th Nov	Routine. T.L.	
16th Nov	Routine T.L.	

PAGE 4

Army Form C. 2118.

WAR DIARY
or
INTELLIGENCE SUMMARY

(Erase heading not required.)

Hour, Date, Place	Summary of Events and Information	Remarks and references to Appendices
BOESCHEPE 17th Nov	Routine as usual T.L.	
18th "	Observation posts — Pte GRICE and Pte JOHNSTON relieved at VOORMEZEELE by Pte BURNS C. and Pte BARTLE J. T.L.	
19th	Operation orders nos. 26 and 27 (24th Division) received regarding move of Div in G. next area. Squadron attached to 17th Bde. for rations during the move but to move independently. T.L.	
20th	Routine T.L.	
21st	Party sent up to DICKEBUSCH to relieve men of observation posts at VOORMEZEELE. Lieut WILSON and 17 other ranks, 5th Corps F.C.P., returned to strength of squadron.	
22nd	1 Sergeant and 12 men returned to strength of Squadron from frontier control posts. Squadron left billets at BOESCHEPE at 4.30 P.M. Proceeded via GODWAERSVELDE —	

PAGE 5

WAR DIARY or INTELLIGENCE SUMMARY

Army Form C. 2118.

Hour, Date, Place	Summary of Events and Information	Remarks and references to Appendices
22nd (Cont.)	STEENVOORT - main CASSEL Road to HARDIFORT. Billeted in 3 farms vacated by 4th Irish Horse. Horses in open. Weather clear with hard frost.	HARDIFORT.
HARDIFORT 23rd Nov.	Forage wagons failed to arrive in time and it was necessary to buy locally oats for midday and evening feeds. Price paid 24 francs per 100 Kilos. Quality Good. Horses turned out into fields for grazing and exercise. T.G. Routine. T.G.	
HARDIFORT 24th Nov. 25th Nov.	Squadron left HARDIFORT at 9.30 a.m. proceeded via WEMAERS CAPPEL - WATTEN- LE BAS to TILQUES. arrived TILQUES 1.30 P.M. Billeted in Sugar factory. All horses under cover except 4 lb. troop and transport. T.G.	

PAGE 6

WAR DIARY
INTELLIGENCE SUMMARY
(Erase heading not required.)

Army Form C. 2118.

Hour, Date, Place	Summary of Events and Information	Remarks and references to Appendices
TILQUES 24th Jan.	Routine as usual T.R.	
" 27th "	Billets in Squar [Square] factory approved by Technical and Boarding School. Men billets found in old chateau between SALPERWICK and ST MARTIN. Squadron moved out to new billets. good Stabling found for all horses in trams[?], rug Parades of Rifle fitting, and training with Drivers to be sent over. All shortages in equipment and clothing to be made good. Programme of work for Squadron sent in to H.Q. Three periods of 1 week each — 1st week individual training. 2nd week - Troop training. 3rd week - Squadron training. Men encouraged to take part in football and Sports.	
SALPERWICK 28th "		

PAGE 7

WAR DIARY
INTELLIGENCE SUMMARY

Army Form C. 2118.

Hour, Date, Place	Summary of Events and Information	Remarks and references to Appendices
SALTERWICK 29th Nov	Routine and individual training. Reinforcement - 5 men having arrived from 3rd line are taken on strength of Headquarters 712. Routine 712.	
30th		

R. Sallow, Capt.

"A" Sqdn S'cas Yeo:
Vol: 4

121/
7911

Army Form C. 2118.

WAR DIARY
or
INTELLIGENCE SUMMARY

(Erase heading not required.)

Instructions regarding War Diaries and Intelligence Summaries are contained in F. S. Regs., Part II. and the Staff Manual respectively. Title pages will be prepared in manuscript.

Hour, Date, Place	Summary of Events and Information	Remarks and references to Appendices
SALPERWICK 1st Dec. 1915	During the time the Squadron is in the rest area, the Squadron is undergoing a period of training and refitting.	
2nd Dec	Billets and stables inspected by General CAPPER commanding 24th Division Staff	
3rd "	Routine	
4th "		
5th "	Lt. C.W. MURRAY having arrived from the 2/1 Glasgow Yeomanry at CUPAR-FIFE, is taken on strength of Squadron this	
6th "	2nd Period of training begun.	
7th "	Troops training under Troop Leaders. Routine	
8th "	Tactical scheme with Divisional cyclists in direction of CARMETTES.	

PAGE 2

WAR DIARY
or
INTELLIGENCE SUMMARY
(Erase heading not required.)

Army Form C. 2118.

Instructions regarding War Diaries and Intelligence Summaries are contained in F. S. Regs., Part II. and the Staff Manual respectively. Title pages will be prepared in manuscript.

Hour, Date, Place	Summary of Events and Information	Remarks and references to Appendices
SALPERWICK		
9th Dec.	Routine Tr.	
10th "	ditto	
11th "	ditto	
12th "	The remount (riding horse) drawn from Divisional teams at ZUDAUSQUES. Tr. Gas Corers & Training defm. Squadron Training Tr.	
13th Dec.		
14th "		
15th "	Routine Tr.	
16th "		
17th "	Sergts Maclean & McNaughton M. on leave to U.K. for one month having rearranged for the duration of the war (Authority G.H.Q memo B 2055 dated 15/1/15) Tr.	

Army Form C. 2118.

WAR DIARY
or
INTELLIGENCE SUMMARY
(Erase heading not required.)

Part 3

Instructions regarding War Diaries and Intelligence Summaries are contained in F. S. Regs., Part II. and the Staff Manual respectively. Title pages will be prepared in manuscript.

Hour, Date, Place	Summary of Events and Information	Remarks and references to Appendices
SALPERWICK 18th Oct 19th " 20th " 21st " 22nd " 23rd.	Routine T.R. Operation order No. 26. 24th Division received orders to take over the line at present held by 4th Div. Squadron to move on 28th November at LEDRINGHEM and move in next day and take up billets vacated by HQ. Division Cavalry. S.Q.M.S. Allan to leave to U.K. for one month's leave in Hungary Sergt Bradley & Cpl Ritchie for duration of the war. (Authority G.H.Q memo B2655 dated 15/4/15) T.R.	

Page 4

Army Form C. 2118.

WAR DIARY
or
INTELLIGENCE SUMMARY

(Erase heading not required.)

Instructions regarding War Diaries and Intelligence Summaries are contained in F. S. Regs., Part II. and the Staff Manual respectively. Title pages will be prepared in manuscript.

Hour, Date, Place	Summary of Events and Information	Remarks and references to Appendices
SAIPERKIEV 24th Dec.	Squadron was formed of Divisional Football competition beating 1st Hunts Staffs. 17th Inf Bde. Troops presented to read plays in the field by General Capper TT.	
25th		
26th & 27th	Order received cancelling operation order No. 28. m Routine	
28th	One hour attached from squadron to HQ to proceed to APM in to assist with Sir Cyclists in Tactical scheme with Sir Cyclists in direction of DIFQUES. Orders received that divisions to take over line held by 17th Division. Squadron to	
29th	proceed to A Squadron HQ at Falke road which is to treated H.A. Squadron will march 17th Brit Cavalry HQ	

1247 W 3299 200,000 (E) 8/14 J.B.C. & A. Form C/2118/11.

WAR DIARY
INTELLIGENCE SUMMARY
(Erase heading not required.)

Army Form C. 2118.

Hour, Date, Place	Summary of Events and Information	Remarks and references to Appendices
SALPER WEEK 30th Dec.	The following men attached to H.Q. for duties in lieu A.P.M.: Cpl. Fraser Pte. Burden " Rae " Kidd " Bogie " Watt " Buchanan " Mcneill J. 78. Routine 75.	
31st		J.M.Murray Capt.

Page 5

CONFIDENTIAL

WAR DIARY
of
"A" Squadron
Q.O.R. Glasgow Yeomanry
from 1.1.16
to 31.1.16.

Vol. 5.   4 pp.

Vol V Page 1

WAR DIARY
or
INTELLIGENCE SUMMARY
(Erase heading not required.)

Army Form C. 2118.

Hour, Date, Place	Summary of Events and Information	Remarks and references to Appendices
ST MARTIN (SALPERWICK) 1st January 1916.	Squadron inspected by General CAPPER.	
2nd " "	Routine	
3rd " "	Routine	
4th " "	Billets cleaned out and arrangements completed for vacating the next area.	
	Lt. Gow, 17 men and 19 horses left for ABEELE for duty as escort to H.Q. 5th Corps.	
	Orders received to send and collect remounts for 24th Divn. at ARNEKE.	
5th " "	Squadron left billets at 9.30 am. Proceeded via ST OMER – ZUYTPEENE – OXELAERE – South of CASSEL and arrived at STEENEVOORDE at 1.30 P.M. Billets there for night. Party collecting remounts from ARNEKE rejoined squadron with 6 Heavy D. Horses and 22 mules. T.G.	
STEENEVOORDE 6th January	at 1.30 P.M. left STEENEVOORDE. 2.30 P.M. arrived at Camp vacated by YORKSHIRE DRAGOONS 17th Divn. 3 miles S.W. of POPERINGHE (Map reference "B" Series Sheet 27 L.11.b.9.5.)	
	Strength Lt. BROWN and Pt. STEVENSON being evacuated sick out of Divisional area, are struck off the strength of squadron T.G.	

WAR DIARY
or
INTELLIGENCE SUMMARY

(Erase heading not required.)

Army Form C. 2118.

Part 2

Instructions regarding War Diaries and Intelligence Summaries are contained in F. S. Regs., Part II. and the Staff Manual respectively. Title pages will be prepared in manuscript.

Hour, Date, Place	Summary of Events and Information	Remarks and references to Appendices
POPERINGHE (Camp 3 miles S.W. of P.) 7th Jan. '16.	Work of making roads and improving camp begun. Strength. Pte. GLENDINNING and Pte. SLOAN having refused to sign on after expiring of their period of service proceeded to Base pending discharge. T.R.	
8th Jan.	Routine	
9th "	Received 24th Divisional operation order No. 32 regarding defence scheme. Strength. Cpl. Brown having returned from hospital is taken on strength of separation.	
10th "	Lt. DONILDSON (Divisional Salvage Officer) and 7 other Ranks proceeded to billets in POPERINGHE. Lance Sergt. Gill and Pte. Robb granted one month's leave having signed on for duration of the war.	
11th "	Inspection of the Camp by G.O.C. T.R.	
12th "	Routine	
13th "	Routine	

WAR DIARY
or
INTELLIGENCE SUMMARY

Army Form C. 2118.

PAGE 3

Hour, Date, Place	Summary of Events and Information	Remarks and references to Appendices
POPERINGHE 1916 14th Jan.	Routine	
15th "	Horses of squadron inoculated - MALLEIN Test.	
16th "	Routine	
17th "	Routine. Strength. Pte. Wadlow having been taken as munition worker, is struck off strength of squadron. 7.8.	
18th "	Routine	
19th "	Routine	
20th "	Routine	
21st "	Major Capper president of Field General Court Martial. Strength 2 horses sent to Mobile Veterinary Section and struck off strength.	
22nd "	Major Capper, president of F.G.C.M. 7.8.	
23rd "	Routine	
24th "	4th men proceed to collect remount at GODEWAERSVELDE for various units of the division. Strength. 2 officers chargers taken on strength. Capt. Galloway left for RENINGHELST for duty as temporary A.P.M. 7.8.	

Page 4

Army Form C. 2118.

WAR DIARY
or
INTELLIGENCE SUMMARY
(Erase heading not required.)

Instructions regarding War Diaries and Intelligence Summaries are contained in F.S. Regs., Part II. and the Staff Manual respectively. Title pages will be prepared in manuscript.

Hour, Date, Place	Summary of Events and Information	Remarks and references to Appendices
POPERINGHE 25th Jan.	Routine. Strength. 11/H. Green proceeded to Base having discharge to commission and is struck off Strength.	T.L.G.
26th Jan.	Routine.	
27th "	Major Cooper president of Court of Inquiry on billet burnt down, 109th B.A.C. R.F.A.	T.L.G.
28th "	Strength. Pte Irving and Pte Gentle proceeded to Base for purpose of undergoing munition worker's test and are struck off Strength of Squadron. Promotions. Saddler Dinneen to be corporal. Pte. Gentleman to be provisional 1/Cpl.	T.L.G.
29th "	Routine.	
30th "	Sergt. Madden, Cpl. Irwin and Cpl. Gilchrist proceeded to YEOMANRY Post (MAP 28. I.17.d.4.0.) for duty as Observation Post. Men to be relieved every 3 days.	T.L.G.
31st "	Routine.	T.L.G.

Confidential

WAR DIARY
of
"A" Squadron Q.O.R. Glasgow Yeomanry
24th Division.
from 1st Feby. to 29th Feby.
1916.

Vol. VI

5 pages.

24

"a" Sp: Pilew Yeo:
Vol: 6

Vol VI Page I

Army Form C. 2118.

WAR DIARY
~~INTELLIGENCE SUMMARY~~

(Erase heading not required.)

Instructions regarding War Diaries and Intelligence Summaries are contained in F. S. Regs., Part II. and the Staff Manual respectively. Title pages will be prepared in manuscript.

Hour, Date, Place	Summary of Events and Information	Remarks and references to Appendices
POPERINGHE (Camp 3 miles SW of P.) 1st Feby 1916	Routine. Strength - one horse being evacuated to Base retaining hospital is struck off strength of squadron	
2nd "	Sergt Taylor attached to escort 5th Corps H.Q.	
3rd "	Oluvactur Post which was posted at YEOMANRY Post on 30th January, moved up to position at HOOGE. Strength. One man evacuated to Base hospital and struck off strength of squadron	
4th "	A second observation post consisting of 3 men sent up to position 2 Kilometres E. of YPRES final. N. of ROULERS Railway. To be called No 2 post, the Hooge post being No 1 post. Reports from these posts to be sent to Divisional H.Q. through the Intelligence Officer of the Brigade occupying the part of the line in which the posts are situated.	
5th "	Sergt Taylor returns to squadron from 5th Corps H.Q. T.H.	

WAR DIARY
INTELLIGENCE SUMMARY

(Erase heading not required.)

Army Form C. 2118.

Instructions regarding War Diaries and Intelligence Summaries are contained in F. S. Regs., Part II. and the Staff Manual respectively. Title pages will be prepared in manuscript.

Hour, Date, Place	Summary of Events and Information	Remarks and references to Appendices
POPERINGHE. July 6th 1916.	Draft. 6 other Ranks having joined from Base are taken on strength of squadron.	
7th	Routine	
8th	Routine	
9th	Routine	
10th	Capt. Gallway & 2 other ranks returned to squadron from detmt. A.P.M. to 24th Division	
11th	Routine	
12th	Very heavy artillery duel all day. At 5.45 P.M. message received from H.Q. "Go alert and stand to." Horses were saddled up and everything got ready to move. At 6.30 P.M. message received cancelling previous order.	
13th	Pte. Bartle on duty with No I observation post reported slight LtLy bombshell. 6.15 P.M. "Stand to" message received from Div. H.Q. 8.50 P.M. message received cancelling "stand to".	
14th	Strength. One man having joined from Base is taken on strength of squad. 2 Horses struck off strength of squadron	T.L.

Army Form C. 2118.

Page 3

WAR DIARY
or
INTELLIGENCE SUMMARY
(Erase heading not required.)

Instructions regarding War Diaries and Intelligence Summaries are contained in F. S. Regs., Part II. and the Staff Manual respectively. Title pages will be prepared in manuscript.

Hour, Date, Place	Summary of Events and Information	Remarks and references to Appendices
Poperinghe Feby. 15th 1916.	4 A.M. Message received from H.Q. "Stand to and move to Sherwood Foresters Pioneer Camp." The alarm sounded. Horses saddled up and transport loaded. Squadron moved off at 6 a.m. and proceeded via POPERINGHE to Sherwood Foresters Camp (2 Kilometers S. of VLAMERTINGHE). Reported to O.C. Sherwood Foresters. Squadron along with Divisional Cyclists and Sherwood Foresters formed divisional reserve which was called out owing to heavy German bombardment and attacks along the line. 9.30 A.M. Message from H.Q. to return to billets. Sergt. McNaughton M. due to return from observation Post No.1 reported missing. Routine.	R.G.
11 P.		

WAR DIARY or INTELLIGENCE SUMMARY

Army Form C. 2118.

Page 4

Instructions regarding War Diaries and Intelligence Summaries are contained in F.S. Regs., Part II. and the Staff Manual respectively. Title pages will be prepared in manuscript.

(Erase heading not required.)

Hour, Date, Place	Summary of Events and Information	Remarks and references to Appendices
POPERINGHE Feby. 17th. 1916	Strength Pte. BARTLE (wounded) brings transfers to No 17 C.C.S. is struck off strength of squadron.	
" 18th.	Routine	
" 19th.	Sergt. M. MACNAUGHTON (previously reported missing) now reported killed while returning from patrol at HOOGE.	
" 20th.	German aeroplane raid at 7.30 a.m. Dropped 13 bombs near camp.	
" 21st.	Taking advantage of clear moon light, German aeroplanes very active. Dropped bombs between ABEELE and POPERINGHE new camp at 1 a.m., & 30 new bombs 6 a.m. Promotions: Lance sergt. Christie to be Sergt. Corpl. Brown to be Lance sergt. Lance corpl. Strachan to be Corporal Pvt. l/cpl. Robertson to be L/cpl. " Pte. Grice to be Prov. L/cpl.	
" 22nd.	Snow and frost. Roads very slippery. Party collected 26 Remounts at GODEWAERSVELDE for various units of Division.	
" 23rd.	Distributed remounts to units.	
" 24th.	A 3rd Observation patrol of 3 men sent to YPRES to report to 73rd Infy Bde at the Ramparts. T.L.S.	

WAR DIARY
INTELLIGENCE SUMMARY
(Erase heading not required.)

Army Form C. 2118.

Hour, Date, Place	Summary of Events and Information	Remarks and references to Appendices
POPERINGHE 25th July 1916	Front Listening Posts Nos 2 and 3 returned to squadron men of to Inf. Bde. to which they were attached coming out of trenches.	
26th July	Routine. Thaw sets in.	
27th	Routine	
28th	Lt. Wilson and 6 O.R. reported to commandant 24th Divl Grenade School to undergo a course of bombing.	
29th	L/Sergt. Brown proceeded to Poperinghe to attend course on "Gas attack". TB.	

Confidential / Vol 7

WAR DIARY 24
of
"A" Squadron A.O.R.
Glasgow Yeomanry
24th Division.

from 1st March
to 31st March 1916.

Volume VIII   5 pages.

Vol. VII Page 1

Army Form C. 2118.

WAR DIARY

INTELLIGENCE SUMMARY

(Erase heading not required.)

Hour, Date, Place	Summary of Events and Information	Remarks and references to Appendices
POPERINGHE 1st March	Observation Post (3 men) sent up to Trench B.4. in SANCTUARY WOOD.	
2nd & 3rd	Nothing to report.	
4th	Orders received from 24th Division to make reconnaissance of area between POPERINGHE - ABEELE - WATOU, and to report on billeting and camping capacity of area with view to forming a rest area for a division. Also to make reconnaissance of roads from area west to CASSEL- WORMHOUDT road.	
5th	Reconnaissance of area begun. Difficulty of reporting on grass field owing to heavy fall of snow.	
6th	French Interpreter (Durocher) recalled from Squadron. T.W.S.	

Army Form C. 2118.

WAR DIARY
INTELLIGENCE SUMMARY
(Erase heading not required.)

Page 1

Instructions regarding War Diaries and Intelligence Summaries are contained in F. S. Regs., Part II. and the Staff Manual respectively. Title pages will be prepared in manuscript.

Hour, Date, Place	Summary of Events and Information	Remarks and references to Appendices
POPERINGHE 7th Mar.	Belgian Interpreter, M. DELMOTTE joined Staadeon	
8th	—	
9th	Report on Reconnaissance of divisional rest area completed and sent to H.Q. The following passed the tests at Divisional Grenade School:- Sergt. Taylor, Cpl. Reeman, 2/Cpl. McLeod, Pte. Fleming, Bruns, Crawford. Lieut. Wilson examination was "good". Capt. Galway proceeded to Div. H.Q. for duty as A.P.M. (temporary)	
10th	—	
11th, 12th & 13th		
14th	Sergt. Brown reported wounded by shrapnel at observation post at HOOGE. T.V.J.	

WAR DIARY

INTELLIGENCE SUMMARY

(Erase heading not required.)

Page 3.

Army Form C. 2118.

Hour, Date, Place	Summary of Events and Information	Remarks and references to Appendices
POPERINGHE 15th	Pte. Barbour reported wounded at observation post in tunnel B.4. SANCTUARY WOOD.	
16th	Capt. Gulvey returned to squadron from duty as acting A.P.M.	
17th, 18th, 19th		
20	Operation order No. 47 received, with regard to 5th Corps relieving Canadian Corps. 24th Div. to be relieved by 3rd Canadian Div. and to move into rest area, with H.Q. at HETRE. Squadron to remain in present billets until 24th Div. moves up into the line in relief of 1st Canadian Div. Horse party sent up to Ramparts at YPRES to meet men of observation posts being relieved owing to move of Division.	

Page 4

Army Form C. 2118.

WAR DIARY
INTELLIGENCE SUMMARY

(Erase heading not required.)

Instructions regarding War Diaries and Intelligence Summaries are contained in F. S. Regs., Part II. and the Staff Manual respectively. Title pages will be prepared in manuscript.

Hour, Date, Place	Summary of Events and Information	Remarks and references to Appendices
POPERINGHE MARCH 21st 22nd 23rd 24th	Nothing to report.	
15th	12 N.C.O's and men left billets to report to O.C. 1st Canadian Div. Mounted Troops in order to take over observation posts from Canadian Div. Cavalry (ALBERTA DRAGOONS)	
26th & 27th		
28th	Orders received for Divisional Mtd. Troops 24th Div. to move to billets being vacated by 1st Canadian Div. Mtd Troops on 31st. 2 miles east of BAILLEUL (Map 28 S.23.A.) Six men proceed to 1st Canadian Div. Mtd Troops for duty at observation posts additional to those sent on 25th.	
29th	Location of posts:- Three on HILL 63, one at ST YVES, one in front line trenches and one on MOUNT KEMMEL.	

Army Form C. 2118.

Page 5

WAR DIARY
INTELLIGENCE SUMMARY
(Erase heading not required.)

Hour, Date, Place	Summary of Events and Information	Remarks and references to Appendices
POPERINGHE 30th Mar.	Advance party proceeded to take over camp from 1st Canadian Divl. Arty. (Troops 2 miles E. of BAILLEUL (map 28 S.23.A)	
BAILLEUL 31st.	Squadron moved off at 2.30 P.M. to new camp. Route: POPERINGHE – HEKSKEN – WESTOUTRE – MOUNT VIDAIGNE. Arrived at camp 5 P.M. T.4.	

Confidential

WAR DIARY

of

"A" Squadron Q.O.R.
Glasgow Yeomanry.

From 1st April
To 30th April 1916

XXIV "A" Janachhu
Vol. 8

Vol. VIII   S Papers

Vol. VIII Page 1

Army Form C. 2118.

WAR DIARY
INTELLIGENCE SUMMARY

(Erase heading not required.)

Hour, Date, Place	Summary of Events and Information	Remarks and references to Appendices
BAILLEUL 1st April 1916.	Five extra men sent up to Observation Posts making 16 men at Hill 63. Two men sent to Post on KEMMEL HILL.	
2nd & 3rd		
4th	Corporal Muir left for G.H.Q. to attend Cadet school prior to being granted commission.	
5th	Two reinforcements arrived from Base.	
6th		
7th	Lieut. Murray & Sergt. Maclean proceeded to FAUQUEMBERGES to attend one week's course on Hotchkiss gun.	
8th	Observation Post rearranged — only 3 posts on Hill 63. Five men for each Post to Observe at night as well as day.	

Page 2

Army Form C. 2118.

WAR DIARY
INTELLIGENCE SUMMARY
(Erase heading not required.)

Instructions regarding War Diaries and Intelligence Summaries are contained in F. S. Regs., Part II. and the Staff Manual respectively. Title pages will be prepared in manuscript.

Hour, Date, Place	Summary of Events and Information	Remarks and references to Appendices
BAILLEUL 9th April	Nothing to report.	
10th "	Orders from Divisional H.Q. to detail 13 mounted men for duty on Frontier Patrol under A.P.M.	
11th "	Two reinforcements arrived from Base and taken on strength of Squadron. One additional man sent to Kemmel post.	
12th "	24th Divisional Defence scheme received. Give all information on the holding of the divisional front and the movements of different units in case of an attack.	
13th "		
14th & 15th "	All leave stopped	G.H.S.

WAR DIARY
INTELLIGENCE SUMMARY
(Erase heading not required.)

Army Form C. 2118.

Page 3

Hour, Date, Place	Summary of Events and Information	Remarks and references to Appendices
BAILLEUL 16th April	Lt. Murray and Sergt. Maclean returned to Squadron from FAUQUEMBERGES (Hotchkiss Gun)	
17th —	All detailed men ordered to return to Squadron took view to preparing for a period of training with 2nd Cavalry division.	
18th —	Men attached to M.M.P. rejoin Squadron.	
19th —	3 reinforcement joined from Base. Divisional escort (5 men & horses) rejoin Squadron	
20th —	Men on obstruction duties (15 from H.H.63 and 3 from Kemmel) rejoin Squadron. Lt. Donaldson (Salvage Officer) and 5 other ranks return to Squadron.	
21st —		
22nd —	5 remounts taken on strength of Squadron. 1 horse (riding) evacuated to 36th mobile veterinary section	

T.4.

WAR DIARY
INTELLIGENCE SUMMARY
(Erase heading not required.)

Page 4

Army Form C. 2118.

Hour, Date, Place	Summary of Events and Information	Remarks and references to Appendices
BAILLEUL 23rd April	Corporal Gordon left for U.K. to Commission.	
24th	Cpl. Ritchie being evacuated to hospital sick on leave in shock off through A Squadron.	
25th	Lieut. Gow & 16 other ranks rejoin Squadron from H.Q. Vth Corps.	
26th	Sergt. Macnaughton left for U.K. to Commission. Squadron along with Cyclists inspected by Major General Capper prior to departure to training area.	
27th	1 Horse evacuated to Base & taken off strength. 4 Horses evacuated to 36th M.V. section. Following promotions made:—	
	To be Sergt. ...... Lance/Sergt. Barlow	
	To be L/Sergt. ... Corporal Sheehan	
	" " Corporal ... L/Corporals Brebin, Kerr, Mackenzie, Hamilton	
	" " L/Cpl. ... Prov: L/Cpl. Litch, Macleod, Gilmour, Gentleman	
	" " Prov. L/Cpl. ... Pte. Paterson, Fleming, Hope, Mackay, U.S.	

Page 5.

Army Form C. 2118.

WAR DIARY
INTELLIGENCE SUMMARY.
(Erase heading not required.)

Hour, Date, Place	Summary of Events and Information	Remarks and references to Appendices
BAILLEUL 28th April. RENESCURE 29th "	Squadron left billets at 10.15 a.m. Marched via BAILLEUL - STRAZEELE - HAZEBROUCK to RENESCURE arriving at 3. P.M. Billeted for the night.	
VAL D'ACQUIN 30th "	Left RENESCURE at 10.30 a.m. Marched via ARQUES - WIZERNES - SETQUES - LUMBRES. Squadron billets at VAL D'ACQUIN. Cyclists at WESTBECOURT.	

T.L. Gallwey

Dear Dean?
for April

www.ingramcontent.com/pod-product-compliance
Lightning Source LLC
Chambersburg PA
CBHW081243170426
43191CB00034B/2020